**Playing with Plays™
Presents
Shakespeare's**

A Midsummer Night's Dream
FOR KIDS
(The melodramatic version!)

For 9-20+ actors, or kids of all ages who want to have fun!
Creatively modified by
Brendan P. Kelso
Cover illustrated by Shana Lopez

3 Melodramatic Modifications to Shakespeare's Play
for 3 different group sizes:

9-10+ actors

11-14+ actors

15-20+ actors

Table Of Contents

Foreword .... Pg 4

School, Afterschool, and Summer classes .... Pg 6

Performance Rights .... Pg 6

9-10+ Actors .... Pg 8

11-14+ Actors .... Pg 26

15-20+ Actors .... Pg 48

Sneak Peeks at other Playing With Plays .... Pg 71

About the Author .... Pg 101

To Cherice;
without her support, dedication, and drive,
I would not have gone this far!

And to the kids who perform,
you make all of this worthwhile!

-Brendan

Playing with Plays™ – Shakespeare's Midsummer Night's Dream for Kids

Copyright © 2004-2020 by Brendan P. Kelso, Playing with Plays LLC

All rights reserved. No part of this book may be reproduced in any form or by any electronic or mechanical means, including photocopying, recording, information storage or retrieval systems now known or to be invented, without permission in writing from the publisher, except by a reviewer, who may quote brief passages in a review, written for inclusion within a periodical. Any members of education institutions wishing to photocopy part or all of the work for classroom use, or publishers who would like to obtain permission to include the work in an anthology, should send their inquiries to the publisher. We monitor the internet for cases of piracy and copyright infringement/violations. We will pursue all cases within the full extent of the law.

Whenever a Playing With Plays play is produced, the following must be included on all programs, printing and advertising for the play: © Brendan P. Kelso, Playing with Plays LLC, www.PlayingWithPlays.com. All rights reserved.

CAUTION: Professionals and amateurs are hereby warned that these plays are subject to a royalty. They are fully protected, in whole, in part, or in any form under the copyright laws of the United States, Canada, the British Empire, and all other countries of the Copyright Union, and are subject to royalty. All rights, including professional, amateur, motion picture, radio, television, recitation, public reading, internet, and any method of photographic reproduction are strictly reserved.

For performance rights please see page 6 of this book or contact:

contact@PlayingWithPlays.com

-Please note, for certain circumstances, we do waive copyright and performance fees. Rules subject to change

www.PlayingWithPlays.com

Printed in the United States of America
Published by Playing With Plays LLC

ISBN-10 099813760-X
ISBN-13: 978-0998137605

Foreword

When I was in high school there was something about Shakespeare that appealed to me. Not that I understood it mind you, but there were clear scenes and images that always stood out in my mind. Romeo & Juliet, "Romeo, Romeo; wherefore art thou Romeo?"; Julius Caesar, "Et tu Brute"; Macbeth, "Double, Double, toil and trouble"; Hamlet, "to be or not to be"; A Midsummer Night's Dream, all I remember about this was a wickedly cool fairy and something about a guy turning into a donkey that I thought was pretty funny. It was not until I started analyzing Shakespeare's plays as an actor that I realized one very important thing, I still didn't understand them. Seriously though, it's tough enough for adults, let alone kids. Then it hit me, why don't I make a version that kids could perform, but make it easy for them to understand with a splash of Shakespeare lingo mixed in? And voila! A melodramatic masterpiece was created! They are intended to be melodramatically fun!

THE PLAYS: There are 3 plays within this book, for three different group sizes. The reason: to allow educators or parents to get the story across to their children regardless of the size of their group. As you read through the plays, there are several lines that are highlighted. These are actual lines from the original book. I am a little more particular about the kids saying these lines verbatim. But the rest, well... have fun!

The entire purpose of this book is to instill the love of a classic story, as well as drama, into the kids.

And when you have children who have a passion for something, they will start to teach themselves, with or without school.

These plays are intended for pure fun. Please DO NOT have the kids learn these lines verbatim, that would be a complete waste of creativity. But do have them basically know their lines and improvise wherever they want as long as it pertains to telling the story. Because that is the goal of an actor: to tell the story. In A Midsummer Night's Dream, I once had a student playing Quince question me about one of her lines, "but in the actual story, didn't the Mechanicals state that 'they would hang us'?" I thought for a second and realized that she had read the story with her mom, and she was right. So I let her add the line she wanted and it added that much more fun, it made the play theirs. I have had kids throw water on the audience, run around the audience, sit in the audience, lose their pumpkin pants (size 30 around a size 15 doesn't work very well, but makes for some great humor!) and most importantly, die all over the stage. The kids love it.

One last note: if you want some educational resources, loved our plays, want to tell the world how much your kids loved performing Shakespeare, want to insult someone with our Shakespeare Insult Generator, or are just a fan of Shakespeare, then hop on our website and have fun:

PlayingWithPlays.com

With these notes, I'll see you on the stage, have fun, and break a leg!

SCHOOL, AFTERSCHOOL, and SUMMER classes

I've been teaching these plays as afterschool and summer programs for quite some time. Many people have asked what the program is, therefore, I have put together a basic formula so any teacher or parent can follow and have melodramatic success! As well, many teachers use my books in a variety of ways. You can view the formula and many more resources on my website at: PlayingWithPlays.com

- Brendan

OTHER PLAYS AND FULL LENGTH SCRIPTS

We have over 25 different titles, as well as a full-length play in 4-acts for theatre groups: Shakespeare's Hilarious Tragedies. You can see all of our other titles on our website here: PlayingWithPlays.com/books

As well, you can see a sneak peek at some of those titles at the back of this book.

And, if you ever have any questions, please don't hesitate to ask at: Contact@PlayingWithPlays.com

ROYALTIES

If you have any questions about royalties or performance licenses, here are the basic guidelines:

1) Please contact us! We always LOVE to hear about a school or group performing our books! We would also love to share photos and brag about your program as well! (with your permission, of course)

2) If you are a group and DO NOT charge your kids to be in this production, contact us about discounted copyright fees (one way or another, we will make this work for you!) You are NOT required to buy a book per kid (but, we will still send you some really cool Shakespeare tattoos for your kids!)

3) If you are a group and DO charge your kids to be in the production, (i.e. afterschool program, summer camp) we ask that you purchase a book per kid. Contact us as we will give you a bulk discount (10 books or more) and send some really cool press on Shakespeare tattoos!

4) If you are a group and DO NOT charge the audience to see the plays, please see our website FAQs to see if you are eligible to waive the performance royalties (most performances are eligible).

5) If you are a group and DO charge the audience to see the performance, please see our website FAQs for performance licensing fees (this includes performances for donations and competitions).

Any other questions or comments, please see our website or email us at:

contact@PlayingWithPlays.com

The 15-Minute or so
A Midsummer Night's Dream

By William Shakespeare
Creatively modified by
Brendan P. Kelso

9-10+ Actors

CAST OF CHARACTERS:

HERMIA: daughter of Egeus and in love with Lysander

LYSANDER: in love with Hermia

HELENA: in love with Demetrius

DEMETRIUS: thinks he is in love with Helena

OBERON: King of the Fairies

PUCK: troublemaker fairy - works for Oberon

TITANIA: Queen of the Fairies

[1]**QUINCE:** leader of the Mechanicals

BOTTOM: lead actor of the Mechanicals

FLUTE: an actor in the Mechanicals

[2]**MECHANICALS:** a group of crazy actors

[1]Quince can be deleted from play if there are only 9 actors, just follow script notes.

[2]Mechanicals can be extra characters if needed.

ACT 1 SCENE 1

HERMIA: Oh....LYSANDER!!!!! *(LYSANDER enters)*

LYSANDER: What's wrong, Hermia?

HERMIA: The Duke said I have three choices: execution, go to a nunnery, or actually listen to my father.

LYSANDER: Why?

HERMIA: My dad wants me to marry Demetrius, bleh...but I want to marry you, Lysander!

LYSANDER: That's all right, Hermia. The course of true love never did run smooth. We'll run off to my Aunt's house. She lives in a place that is far, far, far away and we will go through an enchanted forest in the middle of the night and probably get lost!

HERMIA: Sounds great! *(HELENA enters)*

HELENA: *(depressed)* Oh Hermia, Demetrius loves your beauty. Why can't I be cute like you, then maybe he would love my beauty!

HERMIA: Wow, stinks to be you. Hey, want to know a secret?

HELENA: Yeah!

HERMIA: *(as if whispering in her ear)* Lysander and I are going to run off to his Aunt's house. It's far, far, far away. Promise me you will not tell a single person!

HELENA: Promise! *(HERMIA and LYSANDER exit) (to audience)* Hmmmm....I have a better idea, why don't I let Demetrius know of fair Hermia's flight, and then maybe he will fall in love with me!

(HELENA exits)

ACT 1 SCENE 2

(QUINCE, BOTTOM, and FLUTE enter)

QUINCE (or delete line): Is all our company here?

BOTTOM: FLUTE!!!

FLUTE: What?

BOTTOM: Listen here, Quince, our fabulous director, wants us to perform a play for the Duke and Duchess.

QUINCE (or FLUTE): Great! How about this one, *(takes script from BOTTOM'S hand)* 'The most lamentable comedy, and most cruel death of Pyramus and Thisbe', and we shall call it...... "Pyramus and Thisbe".

BOTTOM: Exactly!

QUINCE (or FLUTE): Great! You play the lead part, Pyramus!

BOTTOM: No, No, No! That's not acceptable! I deserve the best part because I am the best actor!

FLUTE: *(to audience)* More like OVERactor.

BOTTOM: I heard that. *(glaring at Flute)*

QUINCE (or FLUTE): That is the best part.

BOTTOM: Oh, well then.

QUINCE (or BOTTOM): Flute, you will play Thisbe.

FLUTE: *(spoken in a very manly voice)* Great! What is Thisbe? A wandering knight?

QUINCE (or BOTTOM): No, SHE is the lead female part, and you can talk in a small voice.

FLUTE: What?! Did I hear you right? Let me not play a woman; I have a beard coming.

BOTTOM: Fine, let me play Thisbe too!

(starts acting like a girl)

QUINCE (or FLUTE): No. You already have a part, the best part.

BOTTOM: Yeah, yeah.

FLUTE: Do I have to play a girl? This is not good, not good at all.

(ALL exit)

ACT 2 SCENE 1

(PUCK enters)

PUCK: *(to audience)* Just want you all to know that I am a shrewd and knavish sprite call'd Puck. I cause all sorts of trouble. Sometimes I can be a devilish little imp. Yep. That would be me! *(very proud)* Oh look, here comes Titania, Queen of the Fairies, and look over there, it's Oberon, King of the Fairies. He's my boss.

(OBERON and TITANIA enter)

OBERON: *(rude and sarcastic)* Hello.

TITANIA: Goodbye. *(just as rude and sarcastic, and wanting to leave in a hurry)*

OBERON: Wait, please, there is something that I would like to tell you.

TITANIA: What?

OBERON: *(in a sing-song voice)* I don't like you!

TITANIA: *(heavy sarcasm)* Boo hoo, boo hoo hoo.

OBERON: If you give me the treasure I asked for, then I will go with thee.

TITANIA: Not a chance. I'm out of here!

OBERON: *(mocking TITANIA)* I'm out of here!

TITANIA: Bye bye! *(TITANIA exits)*

OBERON: *(very mad)* AAAAGGGGGHHHHH!!!!!!!!!! I have to do something mean to her! *(talking to himself)* What to do? What to do? What to do?

PUCK: *(with a big grin)* So, how can I help?

OBERON: Well, hello my mischievous little friend. I know, go get me the magical purple flower.

PUCK: I'll put a girdle round about the earth in forty minutes. *(PUCK starts to leave)*

OBERON: Huh? *(not understanding what Puck just said)*

PUCK: *(frustrated)* I'll be right back. *(shaking his head and mumbling, PUCK exits)*

(HELENA and DEMETRIUS enter; OBERON watches, unseen)

DEMETRIUS: I love thee not, therefore pursue me not.

HELENA: Demetrius, don't you love me?

DEMETRIUS: No, you bug me, Helena.

HELENA: Even though I told you about Hermia and Lysander running off together?

DEMETRIUS: You still bug me. Now leave me alone… *(shoves HELENA away)*

HELENA: Demetrius, the more you hate me, the more I will love you!

DEMETRIUS: Aghhhhh! Leave me alone! *(HELENA chases DEMETRIUS offstage; PUCK enters)*

PUCK: Your fairy has returned with the magical purple flower!

OBERON: I pray thee, give it me. *(PUCK teases OBERON with flower, then hands over flower)* This is a love potion. I'm going to put some on Titania's eyes. Then she will awake and fall in love with the first thing she sees, hopefully, something filthy and smelly! Puck, you go do something constructive.

PUCK: Constructive?

OBERON: *(frustrated)* I saw a young Athenian couple mad at each other. Use this flower and make them fall in love.

PUCK: Okay!

(PUCK exits; OBERON hides behind a tree)

ACT 2 SCENE 2

(TITANIA enters)

TITANIA: Wow, I'm tired. I think I will fall asleep in the middle of this dark and enchanted forest, while my husband is very, very mad at me.

(TITANIA falls asleep)

OBERON: Well, well, well, looky here! *(OBERON places potion on TITANIA'S eyes)* Wake when some vile thing is near! *(OBERON exits)*

(LYSANDER and HERMIA enter)

LYSANDER: Hmmm, these trees look familiar.

HERMIA: What do you mean by that?

LYSANDER: I have forgot our way.

HERMIA: That's okay. I'm tired. Let's go to sleep.

LYSANDER: Okay.

(LYSANDER and HERMIA lie down and go to sleep)

PUCK: *(PUCK enters and sees LYSANDER lying on the ground)* An Athenian couple, just like the boss said! Pretty soul, how can he be mad at her? A little on each eye and poof, you will now fall in love with the first thing you see!

(places potion on LYSANDER'S eyes; PUCK stands back to watch; DEMETRIUS and HELENA enter)

DEMETRIUS: You are still annoying me, you're like my dog.

HELENA: Then let me be your pet and I will follow you everywhere. *(howls with excitement)*

DEMETRIUS: Nooooooo! Hey, look at that *(points at something off stage in opposite direction, HELENA looks)* I'm outta here! *(DEMETRIUS exits)*

HELENA: Aghhhh, *(Sees LYSANDER lying on the ground, wakes him)* Lysander? Lysander, if you live, good sir, awake. *(HELENA kicks LYSANDER)* I said AWAKE!

LYSANDER: What? *(LYSANDER wakes up totally in love with Helena)*

HELENA: I think Demetrius does not love me.

LYSANDER: And run through fire I will for thy sweet sake.

HELENA: Huh?

LYSANDER: I love you!

HELENA: *(very matter of fact)* But, you love Hermia.

LYSANDER: Not Hermia, but Helena I love: Who would not change a raven for a dove? *(Chasing her, trying to hug and kiss her)* Oh, kiss me, darling!

HELENA: Aghhhhhhhhh! *(HELENA screaming, runs off; LYSANDER chases her)*

(HERMIA wakes up, confused)

HERMIA: Hello? Lysander? Where did you go?

(HERMIA exits other side; PUCK is very amused with the situation)

ACT 3 SCENE 1

(QUINCE, BOTTOM, and FLUTE enter; PUCK is excited that there are new people to watch)

BOTTOM: There are some lines that I think we need to change in the script.

QUINCE (or FLUTE): No, we need to rehearse.

BOTTOM: Okay, I need to warm up first. *(BOTTOM moves over to the side of the stage to "warm up" in some crazy way)*

FLUTE: *(talking out loud to himself)* I wonder if the Thisbe could be a boy? No, no, no....it is a love story.

PUCK: The boss said something smelly and vile, huh? *(PUCK puts a sheet over Bottoms head and pulls him offstage)* I will turn this actor into a donkey! And get the boss' Queen to fall in love with him!!!! Hee, hee, hee.

QUINCE (or FLUTE): *(looking around)* Hey Bottom, where are you?

BOTTOM: *(BOTTOM returns with Donkey head)* Okay, I'm ready!

QUINCE & FLUTE: Aghhhhhhhhhhhhhhhhhhhhhhh!!!!

(ALL see BOTTOM transformed and freak out screaming and yelling anything and everything as they run off stage; TITANIA wakes at this noise and sees BOTTOM)

BOTTOM: Why do they run away? *(feeling his face)* Hey, I think I need to shave.

TITANIA: What angel wakes me from my flowery bed?

BOTTOM: Hey, where did you come from? And who are you?

TITANIA: I awoke to think you are the best-looking person ever! I love thee.

BOTTOM: Whoa! Methinks you should have little reason for that.

(TITANIA grabs BOTTOM'S hand and pulls him off stage)

BOTTOM: Hee-haw!

ACT 3 SCENE 2

(OBERON enters unseen by all but PUCK)

OBERON: So, have you seen my queen?

PUCK: My mistress with a monster is in love. *(very, very, very happy with himself)*

OBERON: Nice! *(DEMETRIUS chasing HERMIA enter)*

DEMETRIUS: How about now?

HERMIA: No. *(more chasing)*

DEMETRIUS: Now?

HERMIA: No! I do not, nor will not like you! Go away! *(shoves him and runs off stage; DEMETRIUS chases her)*

OBERON: *(to PUCK)* You messed it all up! You put the love potion on the wrong Athenian's eyes.

PUCK: I did? Oh well, *(to audience)* but this is very entertaining!

OBERON: *(serious)* This is a problem. *(points for him to leave)*

PUCK: Are you kidding me? This is great entertainment. Just ask the audience. *(to audience)* Hey audience, don't you think this is great entertainment? *(PUCK gets audience to clap and cheer him on; Meanwhile, lovers chasing is still happening)*

OBERON: PUCK! Do something!

(LYSANDER, HELENA, DEMETRIUS, and HERMIA enter)

PUCK: Fine! FREEZE!

(PUCK throws pixie dust on DEMETRIUS; DEMETRIUS suddenly falls madly in love with HELENA)

PUCK: UNFREEZE!

LYSANDER: O Helen, goddess, nymph, perfect, divine! I love you!

HELENA: What? O spite!

DEMETRIUS: *(DEMETRIUS shoves LYSANDER over)* You love her? No! I love thee more!

(LYSANDER and DEMETRIUS start pushing and fighting each other to be noticed by HELENA)

HELENA: Aghhhhhhhhhhh!

HERMIA: *(Upset off to the side)* You thief of love! You took my guy! You took both of my guys!

HELENA: What did you say earlier? Oh, yeah... Stinks to be you.

HERMIA: Oh, yeah? *(HERMIA stomps on HELENA'S foot)*

HELENA: Ouch! *(to audience)* Though she be but little, she is fierce! *(HERMIA chases HELENA off stage; the boys chase HELENA while wrestling with each other; PUCK, again very, very amused at the situation)*

PUCK: Isn't this great!

OBERON: *(very stern)* Puck!

PUCK: I know, I know......*(mocking OBERON)* "This is a problem".

(PUCK pouts, exits chasing foursome)

ACT 4 SCENE 1

(TITANIA and BOTTOM enter)

TITANIA: Can I have my fairy go get you goodies, my sweet love?

BOTTOM: *(Very excited)* Yeah! Have her bring me a candy bar!

OBERON: FREEZE! A donkey, hmmmm. Although this is very funny, I do kind of like her. *(OBERON knocks out BOTTOM, and blows pixie dust on TITANIA'S head)*

OBERON: UNFREEZE!

TITANIA: *(TITANIA awakes like she was in a weird dream)* Oberon, I had a weird dream, you won't believe what happened.

OBERON: Let me guess, you fell in love with a donkey?

TITANIA: *(TITANIA nods her head surprised)* Yeah, how did you know?

OBERON: There lies your love. *(points at BOTTOM)*

TITANIA: Yuck!

OBERON: But, you like me now!

TITANIA: Cool! *(TITANIA and OBERON exit)*

(LYSANDER, HELENA, DEMETRIUS, and HERMIA enter, PUCK follows; ALL are still arguing just like before)

PUCK: FREEZE! *(ALL four freeze in place; PUCK throws pixie dust on DEMETRIUS and faces him towards Helena; Then he throws pixie dust on LYSANDER and faces him towards HERMIA)*

PUCK: UNFREEZE!

LYSANDER: Hermia, I love you.

HERMIA: About time!

DEMETRIUS: Hey Helena, I love you.

HELENA: Finally!

LYSANDER: Hey, I'm tired. Let's go to sleep.

EVERYBODY: Okay.

(they all fall asleep on the ground; PUCK, a little depressed the fun is over, exits; while he exits, he grabs the donkey head from the sleeping BOTTOM; a small amount of time passes then the lovers wakeup)

LOVERS: It was all a dream.

HERMIA: *(to audience)* Oh no! I have to have an answer for the Duke today; execution, nunnery, or listen to my father? Ohhh.... But, I still love Lysander.

DEMETRIUS: And I love Helena.

LYSANDER: Well then Hermia, your dad may be upset, but I think the Duke will be happy we are all in love, and I am sure he will want us all to get married, too! I mean, this is a Shakespeare comedy, right? *(they all nod)* Everybody ALWAYS gets married in a Shakespeare comedy!

LOVERS: Okay! Let's all go get married.

(ALL exit)

ACT 4 SCENE 2

(a candy bar flies on stage and hits Bottom. BOTTOM awakes)

BOTTOM: *(feeling his face)* Methought I was, methought I had….ahhhh, never mind. It must have just been a dream! Oh, look, a candy bar!

(QUINCE and FLUTE enters very depressed)

QUINCE (or FLUTE): *(to audience)* Have any of you seen Bottom?

FLUTE: No?

(BOTTOM walks over)

QUINCE and FLUTE: Bottom!

BOTTOM: Guess what? We get to perform our play in front of the Duke!

QUINCE and FLUTE: Yeah!

(ALL exit)

ACT 5 SCENE 1

(LYSANDER, HERMIA, HELENA, and DEMETRIUS enter)

DEMETRIUS: The Duke couldn't be here tonight, but he said that we were going to watch a play. Helena, what do we have?

HELENA: *(reading from paper)* Listen to this, "A tedious brief scene of young Pyramus and his love Thisbe; very tragical mirth". It is called "Pyramus and Thisbe".

EVERYBODY: Yeah! That sounds great! Where's the popcorn?

(QUINCE, FLUTE and BOTTOM enter, and BOTTOM takes center stage)

QUINCE (or BOTTOM): *(announces play to audience in a deep announcer's voice)* Now presenting, 'Pyramus and Thisbe'.

(ALL applause)

BOTTOM (as Pyramus): I love you, but I can never visit you, so thus die I, thus, thus, thus! Now am I dead. Now die, die, die, die, die.

(PYRAMUS kills himself and dies very, very, very, very dramatically and funny)

FLUTE (as Thisbe): Asleep my love? What, dead, my dove? I must die, too. Adieu, adieu, adieu!

(THISBE kills herself and just falls over; ALL applause while FLUTE and BOTTOM bow and exit)

LYSANDER: Well they couldn't have died soon enough! Time to go to bed. *(ALL exit; PUCK enters and addresses audience)*

PUCK: *(to audience)* If we shadows have offended, think but this, and all is mended. In other words, we really hope you enjoyed our dream. So give me your hands, *(starts clapping)* if we be friends. *(claps with audience)* Goodnight!

(PUCK exits waving to the audience)

THE END

The 20-Minute or so
A Midsummer Night's Dream
By William Shakespeare
Creatively edited by Brendan P. Kelso
11-14+ Actors

CAST OF CHARACTERS:

[1]**EGEUS**: father of Hermia

[2]**THESEUS**: Duke of Athens

[3]**HIPPOLYTA**: Queen of the Amazons – in love with Theseus

HERMIA: daughter of Egeus and in love with Lysander

LYSANDER: in love with Hermia

HELENA: in love with Demetrius

DEMETRIUS: thinks he is in love with Helena

[2]**OBERON**: King of the Fairies

PUCK: troublemaker fairy - works for Oberon

[3]**TITANIA**: Queen of the Fairies

[1]**FAIRY**: works for Titania

QUINCE: leader of the Mechanicals

BOTTOM: lead actor of the Mechanicals

FLUTE: an actor in the Mechanicals

[4]**MECHANICALS**: a group of crazy actors

The same actors can play the following parts:

[1]EGEUS and FAIRY
[2]OBERON and THESEUS
[3]HIPPOLYTA and TITANIA
[4]MECHANICALS can be extra characters if needed

ACT 1 SCENE 1

(HIPPOLYTA and THESEUS enter)

HIPPOLYTA: Theseus, are we getting married yet?

THESEUS: Ahhhh...No.

HIPPOLYTA: Come on, are we getting married yet? *(said like a whiny kid)*

THESEUS: NO.

HIPPOLYTA: Are we getting married yet?!?!

THESEUS: Um, let me think....NOOOOOOOOO!

HIPPOLYTA: Sorry, but I am soooo excited!

THESEUS: Only three days left my dear Hippolyta. Look, here comes Egeus.

(EGEUS and HERMIA enter)

EGEUS: *(frustrated)* Duke, Duchess, I am sooooo mad at my daughter, Hermia!

HIPPOLYTA: Why?

EGEUS: She doesn't want to marry Demetrius.

THESEUS: Hmmmm, come here, Hermia.

HIPPOLYTA: *(to THESEUS)* Be nice to her.

HERMIA: Yes, sir.

THESEUS: You have three choices: execution, go to a nunnery, or actually listen to your father. I want an answer before I get married, got it?

HERMIA: Got it. *(THESEUS, HIPPOLYTA, and EGEUS exit)*

HERMIA: Oh....LYSANDER!!!!! *(LYSANDER enters)*

LYSANDER: What's wrong, Hermia?

HERMIA: My dad wants me to marry Demetrius, bleh...but I want to marry you, Lysander!

LYSANDER: That's all right, Hermia. The course of true love never did run smooth. We'll run off to my Aunt's house. She lives in a place that is far, far, far away and we will go through the enchanted forest in the middle of the night, and probably get lost!

HERMIA: Sounds great! *(HELENA enters)*

HELENA: *(depressed)* Oh Hermia, Demetrius loves your beauty. Why can't I be cute like you, then maybe he would love my beauty!

HERMIA: Wow, stinks to be you. Hey, want to know a secret?

HELENA: Yeah!

HERMIA: *(as if whispering in her ear)* Lysander and I are going to run off to his Aunt's house. It's far, far, far away. Promise me you will not tell a single person!

HELENA: Promise! *(HERMIA and LYSANDER exit)* *(to audience)* Hmmmm....I have a better idea, why don't I let Demetrius know of fair Hermia's flight, and then maybe he will fall in love with me!

(HELENA exits)

ACT 1 SCENE 2

(MECHANICALS enter)

QUINCE: Is all our company here?

MECHANICALS: Yes!

QUINCE: Fabulous! We are going to perform a play before the Duke and Duchess on his wedding day.

MECHANICALS: Yeah!

QUINCE: Our play is 'The most lamentable comedy, and most cruel death of Pyramus and Thisbe', and we shall call it...... "Pyramus and Thisbe".

MECHANICALS: Yeah!

QUINCE: Bottom, you will play Pyramus.

BOTTOM: No, No, No! That's not acceptable! I deserve the best part because I am the best actor!

FLUTE: *(to other mechanicals or audience)* More like OVERactor.

BOTTOM: I heard that. *(glaring at Flute)*

QUINCE: That is the best part. Flute, you will play Thisbe.

FLUTE: *(spoken in a very manly voice)* Great! What is Thisbe? A wandering knight?

QUINCE: No, SHE is the lead female part, and you can talk in a small voice.

FLUTE: What?! Did I hear you right? Let me not play a woman; I have a beard coming.

BOTTOM: Let me play Thisbe too! *(starts acting like a girl)*

QUINCE: No. You already have a part, the best part.

BOTTOM: Yeah, yeah.

QUINCE: That leaves us with Thisbe's mother, the Lion's part, let's see....

BOTTOM: I can play the Lion's part, too! Listen to my lion's roar! *(Bottom starts to roar)*

QUINCE: No. No. NO! You would fright the Duchess and the ladies, that they would shriek; and that were enough to hang us all.

BOTTOM: Man, you are tough! *(as MECHANICALS exit FLUTE says his line)*

FLUTE: Do I have to play a girl? This is not good, not good at all.

(ALL exit)

ACT 2 SCENE 1

(FAIRY enters dancing across stage and singing to herself; PUCK enters but hides from Fairy)

PUCK: Boo!

FAIRY: Aghhh!!!

PUCK: How now, spirit! Whither wander you?

FAIRY: Hey, don't people call you Puck?

PUCK: *(sarcastic)* A very brilliant observation.

FAIRY: Aren't you that shrewd and knavish sprite? Don't you cause all sorts of trouble? Aren't you a devilish little imp?

PUCK: Yep. That would be me! *(very proud)*

FAIRY: Oh look, here comes Titania, Queen of the Fairies. I work for her.

PUCK: Yeah, well here comes Oberon, King of the Fairies. He's my boss. *(OBERON and TITANIA enter)*

OBERON: *(rude and sarcastic)* Hello.

TITANIA: Goodbye. *(just as rude and sarcastic, and wanting to leave in a hurry)*

OBERON: Wait, please, there is something that I would like to tell you.

TITANIA: What?

OBERON: *(in a sing-song voice)* I don't like you!

TITANIA: *(heavy sarcasm)* Boo hoo, boo hoo hoo.

OBERON: If you give me the treasure I asked for, then I will go with thee.

TITANIA: Not a chance. Fairy, let's go! I'm out of here!

FAIRY: Okay.

OBERON: *(mocking TITANIA)* I'm out of here!

TITANIA: Bye bye! *(TITANIA and FAIRY exit)*

OBERON: *(very mad)* AAAAGGGGGHHHHH!!!!!!!!!! I have to do something mean to her! *(talking to himself)* What to do? What to do? What to do?

PUCK: *(with a big grin)* So, how can I help?

OBERON: Well, hello my mischievous little friend. I know, go get me the magical purple flower.

PUCK: I'll put a girdle round about the earth in forty minutes. *(PUCK starts to leave)*

OBERON: Huh? *(not understanding what Puck just said)*

PUCK: *(frustrated)* I'll be right back. *(shaking his head and mumbling, PUCK exits)*

(HELENA and DEMETRIUS enter; OBERON watches, unseen)

DEMETRIUS: I love thee not, therefore pursue me not.

HELENA: Demetrius, don't you love me?

DEMETRIUS: No, you bug me, Helena.

HELENA: Even though I told you about Hermia and Lysander running off together?

DEMETRIUS: You still bug me. Now leave me alone... *(shoves HELENA away)*

HELENA: Demetrius, the more you hate me, the more I will love you!

DEMETRIUS: Aghhhhh! Leave me alone! *(HELENA chases DEMETRIUS offstage; PUCK enters)*

PUCK: Your fairy has returned with the magical purple flower!

OBERON: I pray thee, give it me. *(PUCK teases OBERON with flower, then hands over flower)* This is a love potion. I'm going to put some on Titania's eyes. Then she will awake and fall in love with the first thing she sees, hopefully, something filthy and smelly! Puck, you go do something constructive.

PUCK: Constructive?

OBERON: *(frustrated)* I saw a young Athenian couple mad at each other. Use this flower and make them fall in love.

PUCK: Okay.

(PUCK exits; OBERON hides behind a tree)

ACT 2 SCENE 2

(TITANIA enters with FAIRY)

TITANIA: Wow, I'm tired. I think I will fall asleep in the middle of this dark and enchanted forest, while my husband is very, very mad at me. Fairy!

FAIRY: Yes?

TITANIA: I want you to sing me to sleep.

FAIRY: Sing?

TITANIA: Yes, sing.

FAIRY: Ahhhh, okay......la, la, te da...... la, la, te da...... la, la, te da......la

(TITANIA falls quickly to sleep)

FAIRY: Okay. Sleep tight! *(Titania falls asleep)* Oh, look, a butterfly! *(FAIRY chases it off stage)*

OBERON: Well, well, well, looky here! *(OBERON, places potion on TITANIA'S eyes)* Wake when some vile thing is near! *(OBERON exits)*

(LYSANDER and HERMIA enter)

LYSANDER: Hmmm, these trees look familiar.

HERMIA: What do you mean by that?

LYSANDER: I have forgot our way.

HERMIA: That's okay. I'm tired. Let's go to sleep.

LYSANDER: Okay.

(LYSANDER and HERMIA lie down and go to sleep)

PUCK: *(PUCK enters and sees LYSANDER lying on the ground)* An Athenian couple, just like the boss said! Pretty soul, how can he be mad at her? A little on each eye and poof, you will now fall in love with the first thing you see!

(places potion on LYSANDER'S eyes; PUCK stands back to watch; DEMETRIUS and HELENA enter)

DEMETRIUS: You are still annoying me, you're like my dog.

HELENA: Then let me be your pet and I will follow you everywhere. *(howls with excitement)*

DEMETRIUS: Noooooo! Hey, look at that *(points at something off stage in opposite direction)* I'm outta here! *(DEMETRIUS exits)*

HELENA: Aghhhh, *(Sees LYSANDER lying on the ground, wakes him)* Lysander? Lysander, if you live, good sir, awake. *(HELENA kicks LYSANDER)* I said AWAKE!

LYSANDER: What? *(LYSANDER wakes up totally in love with Helena)*

HELENA: I think Demetrius does not love me.

LYSANDER: And run through fire I will for thy sweet sake.

HELENA: Huh?

LYSANDER: I love you!

HELENA: *(very matter of fact)* But, you love Hermia.

LYSANDER: Not Hermia, but Helena I love: Who would not change a raven for a dove? *(Chasing her, trying to hug and kiss her)* Oh, kiss me, darling!

HELENA: Aghhhhhhhhh! *(HELENA screaming, runs off; LYSANDER chases her)*

(HERMIA wakes up, confused)

HERMIA: Hello? Lysander? Where did you go?

(HERMIA exits; PUCK is very amused with the situation)

ACT 3 SCENE 1

(MECHANICALS enter; PUCK is excited that there are new people to watch)

QUINCE: Are we all met?

BOTTOM: There are some lines that I think we need to change in the script.

QUINCE: No, we need to rehearse.

BOTTOM: Okay, I need to warm up first. *(BOTTOM moves over to the side of the stage to "warm up" in some crazy way)*

FLUTE: Can we talk about this girl part?

QUINCE: Would you just come over here and work on your lines? *(MECHANICALS rehearse together, saying the words "rehearse" several times quietly)*

PUCK: Something smelly, huh? *(PUCK puts a sheet over Bottoms head and pulls him offstage)* I will turn this actor into a donkey! And get the boss' Queen to fall in love with him!!!! Hee, hee, hee.

BOTTOM: *(BOTTOM returns with Donkey head)* Okay, I'm ready!

EVERYBODY: Aghhhhhhhhhhhhhhhhhhhhhhhhhh!!!!

(the MECHANICALS see BOTTOM transformed and freak out screaming and yelling anything and everything as they run off stage; TITANIA wakes at this noise and sees BOTTOM)

BOTTOM: Why do they run away? *(feeling his face)* Hey, I think I need to shave.

TITANIA: What angel wakes me from my flowery bed?

BOTTOM: Hey, where did you come from? And who are you?

TITANIA: I awoke to think you are the best-looking person ever! I love thee.

BOTTOM: Whoa! Methinks you should have little reason for that.

(TITANIA grabs BOTTOM'S hand and pulls him off stage)

BOTTOM: Hee-haw!

ACT 3 SCENE 2

(OBERON enters unseen by all but PUCK)

OBERON: So, have you seen my queen?

PUCK: My mistress with a monster is in love. *(very, very, very happy with himself)*

OBERON: Nice! *(DEMETRIUS chasing HERMIA enter)*

DEMETRIUS: How about now?

HERMIA: No. *(more chasing)*

DEMETRIUS: Now?

HERMIA: No! I do not, nor will not like you! Go away! *(shoves him and runs off stage; DEMETRIUS chases her)*

OBERON: *(to PUCK)* You messed it all up! You put the love potion on the wrong Athenian's eyes.

PUCK: I did? Oh well, *(to audience)* but this is very entertaining!

OBERON: *(serious)* This is a problem. *(points for him to leave)*

PUCK: Are you kidding me? This is great entertainment. Just ask the audience. *(to audience)* Hey audience, don't you think this is great entertainment? *(PUCK gets audience to clap and cheer him on; meanwhile, lovers chasing is still happening)*

OBERON: PUCK! Do something!

(LYSANDER, HELENA, DEMETRIUS, and HERMIA enter)

PUCK: Fine! FREEZE!

(PUCK throws pixie dust on DEMETRIUS; DEMETRIUS suddenly falls madly in love with HELENA)

PUCK: UNFREEZE!

LYSANDER: O Helen, goddess, nymph, perfect, divine! I love you!

HELENA: What? O spite!

DEMETRIUS: *(DEMETRIUS shoves LYSANDER over)* You love her? No! I love thee more!

(LYSANDER and DEMETRIUS start pushing and fighting each other to be noticed by HELENA)

HELENA: Aghhhhhhhhhhh!

HERMIA: *(Upset off to the side)* You thief of love! You took my guy! You took both of my guys!

HELENA: What did you say earlier? Oh, yeah... stinks to be you.

HERMIA: Oh, yeah? *(HERMIA stomps on HELENA'S foot)*

HELENA: Ouch! *(to audience)* Though she be but little, she is fierce! *(HERMIA chases HELENA off stage; the boys chase HELENA while wrestling with each other; PUCK, again very, very amused at the situation)*

PUCK: Isn't this great!

OBERON: *(very stern)* Puck!

PUCK: I know, I know……*(mocking OBERON)* "This is a problem".

(PUCK pouts, exits chasing foursome)

ACT 4 SCENE 1

(TITANIA, BOTTOM, and FAIRY enter)

TITANIA: Can I have my fairy go get you goodies, my sweet love?

BOTTOM: Yeah! *(to FAIRY)* Go get me a candy bar! *(FAIRY exits, mumbling)*

OBERON: FREEZE! A donkey, hmmmm. Although this is very funny, I do kind of like her. *(OBERON knocks out BOTTOM, and blows pixie dust on TITANIA'S head)*

OBERON: UNFREEZE!

TITANIA: *(TITANIA awakes like she was in a weird dream)* Oberon, I had a weird dream, you won't believe what happened.

OBERON: Let me guess, you fell in love with a donkey? There lies your love. *(points at BOTTOM)*

TITANIA: Yuck!

OBERON: But, you like me now!

TITANIA: Cool! *(TITANIA and OBERON exit)*

(LYSANDER, HELENA, DEMETRIUS, and HERMIA enter, PUCK follows; ALL are still arguing just like before)

PUCK: FREEZE! *(ALL four freeze in place; PUCK throws pixie dust on DEMETRIUS and faces him towards Helena; then he throws pixie dust on LYSANDER and faces him towards HERMIA)*

PUCK: UNFREEZE!

LYSANDER: Hermia, I love you.

HERMIA: About time!

DEMETRIUS: Hey Helena, I love you.

HELENA: Finally!

LYSANDER: Hey, I'm tired. Let's go to sleep.

EVERYBODY: Okay.

(they all fall asleep on the ground; PUCK, a little depressed the fun is over, exits; while he exits, he grabs the donkey head from the sleeping BOTTOM; THESEUS, EGEUS enter)

EGEUS: Aghhhhhhhhh! My lord, this is my daughter here asleep!

THESEUS: Yeah, next to some dude and two other Athenians.

EGEUS: Yeah, the wrong dude!

THESEUS: Wake them.

EGEUS: *(EGEUS wakes them)* Hello! What are you doing hanging out with this guy?

LOVERS: It was all a dream.

EGEUS: Yeah, right.

THESEUS: Hermia, do you have your answer? Is it execution, nunnery, or listen to your father?

HERMIA: I still love Lysander.

DEMETRIUS: And I love Helena.

EGEUS: Aghhhhhhhh! *(EGEUS runs off stage in a mad fervor)*

THESEUS: This is great! Let's all go get married.

LOVERS: What?

THESEUS: I mean, this is a Shakespeare comedy, right? *(they all nod)* Everybody ALWAYS gets married in a Shakespeare comedy!

LOVERS: Okay!

(ALL exit)

ACT 4 SCENE 2

(a candy bar flies on stage and hits BOTTOM; BOTTOM awakes)

BOTTOM: *(feeling his face)* Methought I was, methought I had....ahhhh, never mind. It must have just been a dream! Oh, look, a candy bar!

(MECHANICALS enter – depressed)

QUINCE: Has anyone seen Bottom?

FLUTE: No.

QUINCE: *(to audience)* Have any of you seen Bottom?

(BOTTOM walks over)

MECHANICALS: Bottom!

BOTTOM: Guess what? We get to perform our play in front of the Duke!

MECHANICALS: Yeah!

(ALL exit)

ACT 5 SCENE 1

(THESEUS, HIPPOLYTA, EGEUS, LYSANDER, HERMIA, HELENA, and DEMETRIUS enter)

THESEUS: Before our nuptials, we are going to watch a play. Hippolyta, what do we have?

HIPPOLYTA: *(reading from paper)* Listen to this: "A tedious brief scene of young Pyramus and his love Thisbe; very tragical mirth". It is called "Pyramus and Thisbe".

EVERYBODY: Yeah! That sounds great! Where's the popcorn?

THESEUS: *(Yelling off stage)* Bring on the Mechanicals!

(MECHANICALS enter, and QUINCE takes center stage)

QUINCE: *(announces play to audience in a deep announcer's voice)* Now presenting 'Pyramus and Thisbe'.

(ALL applause; QUINCE sits down to side)

BOTTOM (as Pyramus): I love you, but I can never visit you, so thus die I, thus, thus, thus! Now am I dead. Now die, die, die, die, die.

(PYRAMUS kills himself and dies very, very, very, very dramatically and funny)

FLUTE (as Thisbe): Asleep my love? What, dead, my dove? I must die, too. Adieu, adieu, adieu!

(THISBE kills herself and just falls over; ALL applause while MECHANICALS bow and exit)

THESEUS: Well they couldn't have died soon enough! Time to go to bed. *(ALL exit; PUCK enters and addresses audience)*

PUCK: *(to audience)* If we shadows have offended, think but this, and all is mended. In other words, we really hope you enjoyed our dream. So give me your hands, if we be friends. *(claps with audience)* Goodnight!

(PUCK exits waving to audience)

THE END

Notes

The 25-Minute or so
A Midsummer Night's Dream
By William Shakespeare
Creatively edited by Brendan P. Kelso

15-20+ Actors

CAST OF CHARACTERS:

[1]**EGEUS**: father of Hermia

[2]**THESEUS**: Duke of Athens

[3]**HIPPOLYTA**: Queen of the Amazons – in love with Theseus

HERMIA: daughter of Egeus and in love with Lysander

LYSANDER: in love with Hermia

HELENA: in love with Demetrius

DEMETRIUS: thinks he is in love with Helena

OBERON: King of the Fairies

PUCK: troublemaker fairy - works for Oberon

TITANIA: Queen of the Fairies

[5]**PEASEBLOSSOM**: fairy, works for Titania

[5]**COBWEB**: fairy, also works for Titania

[5]**MUSTARDSEED**: fairy, and yes, works for Titania

[5]**MOTH**: yep, another fairy that works for Titania

QUINCE: leader of the Mechanicals

BOTTOM: lead actor of the Mechanicals

FLUTE: an actor in the Mechanicals

[4]**STARVELING**: another actor in the Mechanicals

[4]**SNOUT**: and another actor in the Mechanicals

[4]**SNUG**: you guessed it, an actor in the Mechanicals

The same actors can play the following parts:
[1] EGEUS and FAIRY
[2] THESEUS and OBERON
[3] HIPPOLYTA and TITANIA
[4] SNOUT, STARVELING, and SNUG'S lines can be moved to other Mechanicals to accommodate for number of actors.
[5] FAIRY lines can be combined to one or more fairies to accommodate for number of actors.

ACT 1 SCENE 1

(HIPPOLYTA and THESEUS enter)

HIPPOLYTA: Theseus, are we getting married yet?

THESEUS: Ahhhh...No.

HIPPOLYTA: Come on, are we getting married yet? *(said like a whiny kid)*

THESEUS: NO.

HIPPOLYTA: Are we getting married yet?!?!

THESEUS: Um, let me think....NOOOOOOOOO!

HIPPOLYTA: Sorry, but I am soooo excited!

THESEUS: Only three days left, my dear Hippolyta. Look, here comes Egeus.

(EGEUS and HERMIA enter)

EGEUS: *(frustrated)* Duke, Duchess, I am sooooo mad at my daughter, Hermia!

HIPPOLYTA: Why?

EGEUS: She doesn't want to marry Demetrius.

THESEUS: Hmmmm, come here, Hermia.

HIPPOLYTA: *(to THESEUS)* Be nice to her.

HERMIA: Yes, sir.

THESEUS: You have three choices: execution, go to a nunnery, or actually listen to your father. I want an answer before I get married, got it?

HERMIA: Got it. *(THESEUS, HIPPOLYTA, and EGEUS exit)*

HERMIA: Oh....LYSANDER!!!!! *(LYSANDER enters)*

LYSANDER: What's wrong, Hermia?

HERMIA: My dad wants me to marry Demetrius, bleh...but I want to marry you, Lysander!

LYSANDER: That's all right, Hermia. The course of true love never did run smooth. We'll run off to my Aunt's house. She lives in a place that is far, far, far away and we will go through the enchanted forest in the middle of the night, and probably get lost!

HERMIA: Sounds great! *(HELENA enters)*

HELENA: *(depressed)* Oh Hermia, Demetrius loves your beauty. Why can't I be cute like you, then maybe he would love my beauty!

HERMIA: Wow, stinks to be you. Hey, want to know a secret?

HELENA: Yeah!

HERMIA: *(as if whispering in her ear)* Lysander and I are going to run off to his Aunt's house. It's far, far, far away. Promise me you will not tell a single person!

HELENA: Promise! *(HERMIA and LYSANDER exit)* *(to audience)* Hmmmm....I have a better idea, why don't I let Demetrius know of fair Hermia's flight, and then maybe he will fall in love with me!

(HELENA exits)

ACT 1 SCENE 2

(MECHANICALS enter)

QUINCE: Is all our company here?

MECHANICALS: Yes!

QUINCE: Fabulous! We are going to perform a play before the Duke and Duchess on his wedding day.

MECHANICALS: Yeah!

QUINCE: Our play is 'The most lamentable comedy, and most cruel death of Pyramus and Thisbe', and we shall call it...... "Pyramus and Thisbe".

MECHANICALS: Yeah!

QUINCE: Bottom, you will play Pyramus.

BOTTOM: No, No, No! That's not acceptable! I deserve the best part because I am the best actor!

FLUTE: *(to other mechanicals or audience)* More like OVERactor.

BOTTOM: I heard that. *(glaring at Flute)*

QUINCE: That is the best part. Flute, you will play Thisbe.

FLUTE: *(spoken in a very manly voice)* Great! What is Thisbe? A wandering knight?

QUINCE: No, SHE is the lead female part, and you can talk in a small voice.

FLUTE: What?! Did I hear you right? Let me not play a woman; I have a beard coming.

BOTTOM: Let me play Thisbe too! *(starts acting like a girl)*

QUINCE: No. You already have a part, the best part.

BOTTOM: Yeah, yeah.

QUINCE: Starveling?

STARVELING: Here, Peter Quince.

QUINCE: Starveling, you must play Thisbe's mother.

STARVELING: Huh? I have to play a girl, too?

QUINCE: Tom Snout?

SNOUT: Here, Peter Quince.

QUINCE: You, Pyramus' father. Snug?

SNUG: Here, Peter Quince.

QUINCE: You the Lion's part, and I hope here is a play fitted for the Duke!

SNUG: Ahhh, Quince?

QUINCE: *(impatiently)* Yes.

SNUG: I am slow of study, do you have the script?

QUINCE: Snug, listen buddy, it is nothing but roaring. You will be fine. *(BOTTOM pushes SNUG away)*

BOTTOM: I can play the Lion's part, too! Listen to my lion's roar! *(Bottom starts to roar)*

QUINCE: No. No. NO! You would fright the Duchess and the ladies, that they would shriek; and that were enough to hang us all.

MECHANICALS: That would hang us!

BOTTOM: Man, you are tough! *(as MECHANICALS exit FLUTE and STARVELING say their line)*

FLUTE & STARVELING: Do we have to play girls?

(ALL exit)

ACT 2 SCENE 1

(FAIRIES enter dancing across stage and singing to themselves; PUCK enters but hides from FAIRIES)

PUCK: Boo!

FAIRIES: Aghhh!!!

PUCK: How now, spirit! Whither wander you?

PEASEBLOSSOM: Hey, don't people call you Puck?

PUCK: *(sarcastic)* A very brilliant observation.

COBWEB: Aren't you that shrewd and knavish sprite? Don't you cause all sorts of trouble? Aren't you a devilish little imp?

PUCK: Yep. That would be me! *(very proud)*

MOTH: The one that frights the maidens of the villagery?

PUCK: Again, yes!

MUSTARDSEED: Oh look, here comes Titania, Queen of the Fairies. We work for her.

PUCK: Yeah, well here comes Oberon, King of the Fairies. He's my boss. *(OBERON and TITANIA enter)*

OBERON: *(rude and sarcastic)* Hello.

TITANIA: Goodbye. *(just as rude and sarcastic, and wanting to leave in a hurry)*

OBERON: Wait, please, there is something that I would like to tell you.

TITANIA: What?

OBERON: *(in a sing-song voice)* I don't like you!

TITANIA: *(heavy sarcasm)* Boo hoo, boo hoo hoo.

OBERON: If you give me the treasure I asked for, then I will go with thee.

TITANIA: Not a chance. Fairies, let's go! I'm out of here!

FAIRIES: Okay.

OBERON: *(mocking TITANIA)* I'm out of here!

TITANIA: Bye bye! *(TITANIA and FAIRIES exit)*

OBERON: *(very mad)* AAAAGGGGGHHHHH!!!!!!!!!! I have to do something mean to her! *(talking to himself)* What to do? What to do? What to do?

PUCK: *(with a big grin)* So, how can I help?

OBERON: Well, hello my mischievous little friend. I know, go get me the magical purple flower.

PUCK: I'll put a girdle round about the earth in forty minutes. *(PUCK starts to leave)*

OBERON: Huh? *(not understanding what Puck just said)*

PUCK: *(frustrated)* I'll be right back. *(shaking his head and mumbling, PUCK exits)*

(HELENA and DEMETRIUS enter; OBERON watches, unseen)

DEMETRIUS: I love thee not, therefore pursue me not.

HELENA: Demetrius, don't you love me?

DEMETRIUS: No, you bug me, Helena.

HELENA: Even though I told you about Hermia and Lysander running off together?

DEMETRIUS: You still bug me. Now leave me alone... *(shoves HELENA away)*

HELENA: Demetrius, the more you hate me, the more I will love you!

DEMETRIUS: Aghhhhh! Leave me alone! *(HELENA chases DEMETRIUS offstage; PUCK enters)*

PUCK: Your fairy has returned with the magical purple flower!

OBERON: I pray thee, give it me. *(PUCK teases OBERON with flower, then hands over flower)* This is a love potion. I'm going to put some on Titania's eyes. Then she will awake and fall in love with the first thing she sees, hopefully, something filthy and smelly! Puck, you go do something constructive.

PUCK: Constructive?

OBERON: *(frustrated)* I saw a young Athenian couple mad at each other. Use this flower and make them fall in love.

PUCK: Okay.

(PUCK exits; OBERON hides behind a tree)

ACT 2 SCENE 2

(TITANIA enters with FAIRIES)

TITANIA: Wow, I'm tired. I think I will fall asleep in the middle of this dark and enchanted forest, while my husband is very, very mad at me. Fairies!

FAIRIES: Yes?

TITANIA: I want you to sing me to sleep.

FAIRIES: Sing?

TITANIA: Yes, sing.

FAIRIES: Ahhhh, okay......la, la, te da...... la, la, te da...... la, la, te da......la

(TITANIA falls quickly to sleep)

FAIRIES: Okay. Sleep tight! *(Titania falls asleep)* Oh, look, butterflies! *(FAIRIES chase them off stage)*

OBERON: Well, well, well, looky here! *(OBERON, places potion on TITANIA'S eyes)* Wake when some vile thing is near! *(OBERON exits)*

(LYSANDER and HERMIA enter)

LYSANDER: Hmmm, these trees look familiar.

HERMIA: What do you mean by that?

LYSANDER: I have forgot our way.

HERMIA: That's okay. I'm tired. Let's go to sleep.

LYSANDER: Okay.

(LYSANDER and HERMIA lie down and go to sleep)

PUCK: *(PUCK enters and sees LYSANDER lying on the ground)* An Athenian couple, just like the boss said! Pretty soul, how can he be mad at her? A little on each eye and poof, you will now fall in love with the first thing you see!

(places potion on LYSANDER'S eyes; PUCK stands back to watch; DEMETRIUS and HELENA enter running)

DEMETRIUS: You are still annoying me, you're like my dog.

HELENA: Then let me be your pet and I will follow you everywhere. *(howls with excitement)*

DEMETRIUS: Nooooooo! Hey, look at that *(points at something off stage in opposite direction)* I'm outta here! *(DEMETRIUS exits)*

HELENA: Aghhhh. *(Sees LYSANDER lying on the ground, wakes him)* Lysander? Lysander, if you live, good sir, awake. *(HELENA kicks LYSANDER)* I said AWAKE!

LYSANDER: What? *(LYSANDER wakes up totally in love with Helena)*

HELENA: I think Demetrius does not love me.

LYSANDER: And run through fire I will for thy sweet sake.

HELENA: Huh?

LYSANDER: I love you!

HELENA: *(very matter of fact)* But, you love Hermia.

LYSANDER: Not Hermia, but Helena I love: Who would not change a raven for a dove? *(Chasing her, trying to hug and kiss her)* Oh, kiss me, darling!

HELENA: Aghhhhhhhhh! *(HELENA screaming, runs off; LYSANDER chases her)*

(HERMIA wakes up, confused)

HERMIA: Hello? Lysander? Where did you go?

(HERMIA exits; PUCK is very amused with the situation)

ACT 3 SCENE 1

(MECHANICALS enter; PUCK is excited that there are new people to watch)

QUINCE: Are we all met?

BOTTOM: There are some lines that I think we need to change in the script.

QUINCE: No, we need to rehearse.

BOTTOM: Okay, I need to warm up first. *(BOTTOM moves over to the side of the stage to "warm up" in some crazy way)*

FLUTE: Can we talk about this girl part?

STARVELING: Yeah!

QUINCE: Would you just come over here and work on your lines? *(MECHANICALS rehearse together, saying the words "rehearse" several times quietly)*

PUCK: Something smelly, huh? *(PUCK puts a sheet over Bottoms head and pulls him offstage)* I will turn this actor into a donkey! And get the boss' Queen to fall in love with him!!!! Hee, hee, hee.

BOTTOM: *(BOTTOM returns with Donkey head)* Okay, I'm ready!

EVERYBODY: Aghhhhhhhhhhhhhhhhhhhhhhhhhhh!!!!

(the MECHANICALS see BOTTOM transformed and freak out screaming and yelling anything and everything as they run off stage; TITANIA wakes at this noise and sees BOTTOM)

BOTTOM: Why do they run away? *(feeling his face)* Hey, I think I need to shave.

TITANIA: What angel wakes me from my flowery bed?

BOTTOM: Hey, where did you come from? And who are you?

TITANIA: I awoke to think you are the best-looking person ever! I love thee.

BOTTOM: Whoa! Methinks you should have little reason for that.

(TITANIA grabs BOTTOM'S hand and pulls him off stage)

BOTTOM: Hee-haw!

ACT 3 SCENE 2

(OBERON enters unseen by all but PUCK)

OBERON: So, have you seen my queen?

PUCK: My mistress with a monster is in love. *(very, very, very happy with himself)*

OBERON: Nice! *(DEMETRIUS chasing HERMIA enter)*

DEMETRIUS: How about now?

HERMIA: No. *(more chasing)*

DEMETRIUS: Now?

HERMIA: No! I do not, nor will not like you! Go away! *(shoves him and runs off stage; DEMETRIUS chases her)*

OBERON: *(to PUCK)* You messed it all up! You put the love potion on the wrong Athenian's eyes.

PUCK: I did? Oh well, *(to audience)* but this is very entertaining!

OBERON: *(serious)* This is a problem. *(points for him to leave)*

PUCK: Are you kidding me? This is great entertainment. Just ask the audience. *(to audience)* Hey audience, don't you think this is great entertainment? *(PUCK gets audience to clap and cheer him on; meanwhile, lovers chasing is still happening)*

OBERON: PUCK! Do something!

(LYSANDER, HELENA, DEMETRIUS, and HERMIA enter)

PUCK: Fine! FREEZE!

(PUCK throws pixie dust on DEMETRIUS; DEMETRIUS suddenly falls madly in love with HELENA)

PUCK: UNFREEZE!

LYSANDER: O Helen, goddess, nymph, perfect, divine! I love you!

HELENA: What? O spite!

DEMETRIUS: *(DEMETRIUS shoves LYSANDER over)* You love her? No! I love thee more!

(LYSANDER and DEMETRIUS start pushing and fighting each other saying, "mine, mine, mine" to be noticed by HELENA)

HELENA: Aghhhhhhhhhhh!

HERMIA: *(Upset off to the side)* You thief of love! You took my guy! You took both of my guys!

HELENA: What did you say earlier? Oh, yeah... stinks to be you.

HERMIA: Oh, yeah? *(HERMIA stomps on HELENA'S foot)*

HELENA: Ouch! *(to audience)* Though she be but little, she is fierce! *(HERMIA chases HELENA off stage; the boys chase HELENA while wrestling with each other; PUCK, again very, very amused at the situation)*

PUCK: Isn't this great!

OBERON: *(very stern)* Puck!

PUCK: I know, I know......*(mocking OBERON)* "This is a problem".

(PUCK pouts, exits chasing foursome)

ACT 4 SCENE 1

(TITANIA, BOTTOM, and FARIES enter)

TITANIA: Can I have my fairies go get you goodies, my sweet love?

BOTTOM: Yeah! *(to the FARIES)* Go get me a candy bar! *(FARIES exit, mumbling)*

OBERON: FREEZE! A donkey, hmmmm. Although this is very funny, I do kind of like her. *(OBERON nocks out BOTTOM, and blows pixie dust on TITANIA'S head)*

OBERON: UNFREEZE!

TITANIA: *(TITANIA awakes like she was in a weird dream)* Oberon, I had a weird dream, you won't believe what happened.

OBERON: Let me guess, you fell in love with a donkey? There lies your love. *(points at BOTTOM)*

TITANIA: Yuck!

OBERON: But, you like me now!

TITANIA: Cool! *(TITANIA and OBERON exit)*

(LYSANDER, HELENA, DEMETRIUS, and HERMIA enter, PUCK follows; ALL are still arguing just like before)

PUCK: FREEZE! *(ALL four freeze in place; PUCK throws pixie dust on DEMETRIUS and faces him towards Helena; then he throws pixie dust on LYSANDER and faces him towards HERMIA)*

PUCK: UNFREEZE!

LYSANDER: Hermia, I love you.

HERMIA: About time!

DEMETRIUS: Hey Helena, I love you.

HELENA: Finally!

LYSANDER: Hey, I'm tired. Let's go to sleep.

EVERYBODY: Okay.

(they all fall asleep on the ground; PUCK, a little depressed the fun is over, exits; while he exits, he grabs the donkey head from the sleeping BOTTOM; THESEUS, EGEUS enter)

EGEUS: Aghhhhhhhh! My lord, this is my daughter here asleep!

THESEUS: Yeah, next to some dude and two other Athenians.

EGEUS: Yeah, the wrong dude!

THESEUS: Wake them.

EGEUS: *(EGEUS wakes them)* Hello! What are you doing hanging out with this guy?

LOVERS: It was all a dream.

EGEUS: Yeah, right.

THESEUS: Hermia, do you have your answer? Is it execution, nunnery, or listen to your father?

HERMIA: I still love Lysander.

DEMETRIUS: And I love Helena.

EGEUS: Aghhhhhhhh! *(EGEUS runs off stage in a mad fervor)*

THESEUS: This is great! Let's all go get married.

LOVERS: What?

THESEUS: I mean, this is a Shakespeare comedy, right? *(they all nod)* Everybody ALWAYS gets married in a Shakespeare comedy!

LOVERS: Okay!

(ALL exit)

ACT 4 SCENE 2

(a candy bar flies on stage and hits BOTTOM; BOTTOM awakes)

BOTTOM: *(feeling his face)* Methought I was, methought I had….ahhhh, never mind. It must have just been a dream! Oh, look, a candy bar!

(MECHANICALS enter – depressed)

QUINCE: Has anyone seen Bottom?

MECHANICALS: No.

QUINCE: *(to audience)* Have any of you seen Bottom?

(BOTTOM walks over)

MECHANICALS: Bottom!

BOTTOM: Guess what? We get to perform our play in front of the Duke!

MECHANICALS: Yeah!

(ALL exit)

ACT 5 SCENE 1

(THESEUS, HIPPOLYTA, EGEUS, LYSANDER, HERMIA, HELENA, and DEMETRIUS enter)

THESEUS: Before our nuptials, we are going to watch a play. Hippolyta, what do we have?

HIPPOLYTA: *(reading from paper)* Listen to this: "A tedious brief scene of young Pyramus and his love Thisbe; very tragical mirth". It is called "Pyramus and Thisbe".

EGEUS: Wait! It is a REALLY lousy play. It's only some ten words long, and, in my humble opinion, about ten words too long.

THESEUS: Thanks for your opinion, Egeus, but, we will hear it.

EGEUS: Fine.

EVERYBODY: Yeah! That sounds great! Where's the popcorn?

THESEUS: *(Yelling off stage)* Bring on the Mechanicals! Time for the ol' Shakespeare play-within-a-play.

(MECHANICALS enter and sit to side; QUINCE takes center stage)

QUINCE: *(announces play to audience in a deep announcer's voice)* Now presenting 'Pyramus and Thisbe'.

(ALL applause; QUINCE sits down to side; SNOUT, BOTTOM, and FLUTE to center stage)

SNOUT: *(to audience standing with his arms out to side)* I, Snout by name, am a wall. This is Pyramus *(motions to BOTTOM)* and Thisbe. *(motions to FLUTE)*

DEMETRIUS: A talking wall, sweet!

BOTTOM: *(as Pyramus and very melodramatically)* My love Thisbe, I love you, but can never be with you, because of this wicked wall!

FLUTE: *(as Thisbe and very melodramatically)* My love Pyramus... I know.

HERMIA: Short but powerful, I like her!

(SNOUT, BOTTOM, and FLUTE move to side of stage; SNUG and STARVELING to center stage)

SNUG: I, Snug the joiner, am a lion! But, I am a soft and nice lion, so I don't scare the ladies.

LYSANDER: And a nice lion, bravo!

STARVELING: *(holding a flashlight)* And I am moonshine! I shine... moonlight. *(flashing light into audience; QUINCE runs on and shows STARVELING how to point light at actors)*

FLUTE: *(center stage as Thisbe)* Where is my...

SNUG: *(as lion, and softly)* Roar...

FLUTE: *(as Thisbe)* Aghhhhh!!!! *(screams running offstage, FLUTE and SNUG sit to side)*

DEMETRIUS: Well roared, Lion.

HELENA: Well run, Thisbe.

STARVELING: This part stinks!

QUINCE: Shhhh!!!

BOTTOM: *(to center stage as Pyramus)* What? Lion hath taken my love?! NOOOOOOO!!! I love you, but I can never visit you, so thus die I, thus, thus, thus! Now am I dead. Now die, die, die, die, die.

(PYRAMUS kills himself and dies very, very, very, very dramatically and funny)

FLUTE: *(to center stage as Thisbe)* Asleep my love? What, dead, my dove? I must die, too. Adieu, adieu, adieu!

(THISBE kills herself and just falls over; ALL applause while MECHANICALS bow and exit)

THESEUS: Well they couldn't have died soon enough! Time to go to bed. *(ALL exit; PUCK enters and addresses audience)*

PUCK: *(to audience)* If we shadows have offended, think but this, and all is mended. In other words, we really hope you enjoyed our dream. So give me your hands, if we be friends. *(claps with audience)* Goodnight!

(PUCK exits waving to audience)

THE END

Sneak Peeks at other Playing With Plays books:

Jungle Book for Kids .... Pg 72

Hamlet for Kids .... Pg 73

Two Gentlemen of Verona for Kids .... Pg 76

The Three Musketeers for Kids .... Pg 79

Christmas Carol for Kids .... Pg 81

Treasure Island for Kids .... Pg 84

Tempest for Kids .... Pg 86

King Lear for Kids .... Pg 88

Macbeth for Kids .... Pg 91

Taming of the Shrew for Kids .... Pg 93

Oliver Twist for Kids .... Pg 96

Much Ado About Nothing for Kids .... Pg 99

Sneak peek of
The Jungle Book for Kids

PARENT WOLF: Oh hi, Bagheera. What's happening in the life of a panther?

BAGHEERA: I wanted to warn you. Shere Khan's in town again.

PARENT WOLF: The tiger? What's he doing in this part of the jungle?

BAGHEERA: What tigers do. You know, hunt, eat, hunt again, eat... hunt...eat... *(trailing off)*

PARENT WOLF: *(play-acting like a tiger)* Oh look at me, I'm a mean ol' tiger, roar!!! *(there is a LOUD ROAR and GROWL from offstage, PARENT WOLF is a bit shocked)*

BAGHEERA: Listen! That's him now!

(enter MOWGLI, running off-balance, and falling down)

PARENT WOLF: Whoa! A man's cub! Look! *(ALL turn to look at MOWGLI)* How little and so... smelly, but cute! *(starts petting his hair)*

(BAGHEERA sneaks over to MOWGLI and whispers something in his ear. MOWGLI sighs and gets down on his knees to appear smaller; he remains on his knees throughout the rest of the scene and ACT1 SCENE 2)

MOWGLI: *(very sarcastically)* Gaa gaa. Goo goo.

(SHERE KHAN enters. PARENT WOLF hides MOWGLI behind her back)

SHERE KHAN: A man's cub went this way. Its parents have run off. Give it to me. I'll uh... take care of him... *(as he rubs his belly)* you can TOTALLY trust me! *(gives* *the audience a big evil smile)*

PARENT WOLF: You are NOT the boss of us.

SHERE KHAN: Excuse me?! Do you know who I am? It is I, Shere Khan, who speaks! I'm kind of a big deal. And scary! GRRRRR.

PARENT WOLF: The man's cub is mine; he shall not be killed! So beat it; you don't scare us.

SHERE KHAN: Fine. But I'll get him some day, make no mistake! Muahahahahaha! ROAR! *(SHERE KHAN exits)*

PARENT WOLF: *(to MOWGLI)* Mowgli the Frog I will call thee. Lie still, little frog.

MOWGLI: *(to PARENT WOLF)* Frog?

PARENT WOLF: *(to MOWGLI and audience)* Yeah, I guess Rudyard Kipling liked frogs! But now we have to see what the wolf leader says.

(enter AKELA, BAGHEERA, and BALOO)

AKELA: Okay, wolves, let's get this meeting started! Howl!

WOLVES: Howl!! *(ALL WOLVES howl)*

PARENT WOLF: Akela, our great leader, I'd like to present the newest member of our pack, Mowgli the Frog!

AKELA: Hmmm, Frog, huh? If you say so.

(enter SHERE KHAN)

SHERE KHAN: ROAR! The cub is mine! Give him to me!

AKELA: Who speaks for this cub?

BALOO: *(speaking in a big, deep bear voice!)* I, Baloo the Bear, I speak for the man's cub. I myself will teach him the ways of the jungle.

Sneak peek of
Hamlet for Kids

(enter GERTRUDE and POLONIUS)

GERTRUDE: What's up, Polonius?

POLONIUS: I am going to hide and spy on your conversation with Hamlet!

GERTRUDE: Oh, okay.

(POLONIUS hides somewhere, enter HAMLET very mad, swinging his sword around)

HAMLET: MOM!!! I AM VERY MAD!

GERTRUDE: Ahhh! You scared me!

(POLONIUS sneezes from hiding spot)

HAMLET: *(not seeing POLONIUS)* How now, a rat? Who's hiding? *(stabs POLONIUS)*

POLONIUS: O, I am slain! Ohhhh the pain! *(dies on stage)*

GERTRUDE: Oh me, what has thou done?

HAMLET: Oops, I thought that was Claudius. Hmph, oh well... as I was saying, I AM MAD you married uncle Claudius!

GERTRUDE: Oh that, yeah, sorry. *(in a motherly voice)* Now, you just killed Polonius, clean up this mess and go to your room!

HAMLET: Okay Mom.

(ALL exit, HAMLET drags POLONIUS' body offstage)

ACT 4 SCENES 1-3

(enter GERTRUDE and CLAUDIUS)

GERTRUDE: Ahhh, Dear?

CLAUDIUS: Yeah?

GERTRUDE: Ummmm, you would not believe what I have seen tonight! Polonius is dead.

CLAUDIUS: WHAT!?

GERTRUDE: Yeah, Hamlet was acting a little crazy, Polonius sneezed or something, then Hamlet yelled, "A rat, a rat!" and then WHACK! It was over.

CLAUDIUS: *(very angry)* HAMLET!!!! GET OVER HERE NOW!!!!!

(enter HAMLET)

CLAUDIUS: *(very casual)* Hey, what's up?

HAMLET: What noise, who calls on Hamlet? What do you want?

CLAUDIUS: Now, Hamlet. Where's Polonius' body?

HAMLET: I'm not telling!

CLAUDIUS: Oh come on, please tell me!!! Please! With a cherry on top! Where is Polonius?

HAMLET: Oh, all right. He's over there, up the stairs into the lobby. *(points offstage)*

(POLONIUS enters and dies again)

CLAUDIUS: Ewe... he's a mess! Hamlet, I am sending you off to England.

HAMLET: Fine! Farewell, dear Mother. And I'm taking this with me! *(HAMLET grabs POLONIUS and drags him offstage)*

(ALL exit but CLAUDIUS)

CLAUDIUS: *(to audience)* I have arranged his execution in England! *(laughs evilly as he exits)* Muwahahaha...

Sneak peek of
Two Gentlemen of Verona for Kids

ANTONIO: It's not nothing.

PROTEUS: Ahhhhh......It's a letter from Valentine, telling me what a great time he's having in Milan, yeah... that's what it says!

ANTONIO: Awesome! Glad to hear it! Because, you leave tomorrow to join Valentine in Milan.

PROTEUS: What!? Dad! No way! I don't want... I mean, I need some time. I've got some things to do.

ANTONIO: Like what?

PROTEUS: You know...things! Important things! And stuff! Lots of stuff!

ANTONIO: No more excuses! Go pack your bag. *(ANTONIO begins to exit)*

PROTEUS: Fie!

ANTONIO: What was that?

PROTEUS: Fiiii......ne with me, Pops! *(ANTONIO exits)* I was afraid to show my father Julia's letter, lest he should take exceptions to my love; and my own lie of an excuse made it easier for him to send me away.

ANTONIO: *(Offstage)* Proteus! Get a move on!!

PROTEUS: Fie!!!

(exit)

ACT 2 SCENE 1

(enter VALENTINE and SPEED following)

VALENTINE: Ah, Silvia, Silvia! *(heavy sighs)*

SPEED: *(mocking)* Madam Silvia! Madam Silvia! Gag me.

VALENTINE: Knock it off! You don't know her.

SPEED: Do too. She's the one that you can't stop staring at. Makes me wanna barf.

VALENTINE: I do not stare!

SPEED: You do. AND you keep singing that silly love song. *(sing INSERT SAPPY LOVE SONG)* You used to be so much fun.

VALENTINE: Huh? *(heavy sigh, starts humming SAME LOVE SONG)*

SPEED: Never mind.

VALENTINE: I have loved her ever since I saw her. Here she comes!

SPEED: Great. *(to audience)* Watch him turn into a fool.

(enter SILVIA)

VALENTINE: Hey, Silvia.

SILVIA: Hey, Valentine. What's goin' on?

VALENTINE: Nothin'. What's goin' on with you?

SILVIA: Nothin'.

(pause)

VALENTINE: What are you doing later?

SILVIA: Not sure. Prob-ly nothin'. You?

VALENTINE: Me neither. Nothin'.

SILVIA: Yea?

VALENTINE: Probably.

SPEED: *(to audience)* Kill me now.

SILVIA: Well, I guess I better go.

VALENTINE: Oh, okay! See ya'..

(pause)

SILVIA: See ya' later maybe?

VALENTINE: Oh, yea! Maybe! Yea! Okay!

SILVIA: Bye.

VALENTINE: Bye!

(exit SILVIA)

SPEED: *(aside)* Wow. *(to VALENTINE)* Dude, what the heck was that?

VALENTINE: I think she has a boyfriend. I can tell.

SPEED: Dude! She is so into you! How could you not see that?

VALENTINE: Do you think?

SPEED: Come on. We'll talk it through over dinner. *(to audience)* Fool. Am I right?

(exit)

Sneak peek of
The Three Musketeers for Kids

(ATHOS and D'ARTAGNAN enter)

ATHOS: Glad you could make it. I have engaged two of my friends as seconds.

D'ARTAGNAN: Seconds?

ATHOS: Yeah, they make sure we fight fair. Oh, here they are now!

(enter ARAMIS and PORTHOS singing, "Bad boys, bad boys, watcha gonna do...")

PORTHOS: Hey! I'm fighting him in an hour. I am going to fight... because...well... I am going to fight!

ARAMIS: And I fight him at two o'clock! Ours is a theological quarrel. *(does a thinking pose)*

D'ARTAGNAN: Yeah, yeah, yeah... I'll get to you soon!

ATHOS: We are the Three Musketeers; Athos, Porthos, and Aramis.

D'ARTAGNAN: Whatever, Ethos, Pathos, and Logos, let's just finish this! *(swords crossed and are about to fight; enter JUSSAC and cardinal's guards)*

PORTHOS: The cardinal's guards! Sheathe your swords, gentlemen.

JUSSAC: Dueling is illegal! You are under arrest!

ARAMIS: *(to ATHOS and PORTHOS)* There are five of them and we are but three.

D'ARTAGNAN: *(steps forward to join them)* It appears to me we are four! I have the spirit; my heart is that of a Musketeer.

PORTHOS: Great! I love fighting!

(Musketeers say "Fight, fight fight!...Fight, fight, fight!" as they are fighting; D'ARTAGNAN fights JUSSAC and it's the big fight; JUSSAC is wounded and exits; the 3 MUSKETEERS cheer)

ATHOS: Well done! Let's go see Treville and the king!

ARAMIS: And we don't have to kill you now!

PORTHOS: And let's get some food, too! I'm hungry!

D'ARTAGNAN: *(to audience)* This is fun!

(ALL exit)

ACT 2 SCENE 1

(enter 3 MUSKETEERS, D'ARTAGNAN, and TREVILLE)

TREVILLE: The king wants to see you, and he's not too happy you killed a few of the cardinal's guards.

(enter KING)

KING: *(yelling)* YOU GUYS HUMILIATED THE CARDINAL'S GUARDS!

ATHOS: Sire, they attacked us!

KING: Oh...Well then, bravo! I hear D'Artagnan beat the cardinal's best swordsman! Brave young man! Here's some money for you. Enjoy! *(hands money to D'ARTAGNAN)*

D'ARTAGNAN: Sweet!

(ALL exit)

Sneak peek of
Christmas Carol for Kids

(enter GHOST PRESENT wearing a robe and holding a turkey leg and a goblet)

GHOST PRESENT: Wake up, Scrooge! I am the Ghost of Christmas Present. Look upon me!

SCROOGE: I'm looking. Not that impressed. But let's get on with it.

GHOST PRESENT: Touch my robe! *(SCROOGE touches GHOST PRESENT's robe. Pause. They look at each other)* Er...it must be broken. Guess we walk. Come on. *(they begin walking downstage)*

SCROOGE: Where are we going?

GHOST PRESENT: Your employee, Bob Cratchit's house. Oh look, here we are.

(enter BOB, MRS. CRATCHIT, MARTHA CRATCHIT, and TINY TIM, who has a crutch in one hand; they are all holding bowls)

BOB: *(to audience)* Hi, we're the Cratchit family. We are a REALLY happy family!

MRS. CRATCHIT: *(to audience)* Yes, but we're REALLY poor, too. Thanks to HIS boss! *(pointing at BOB)*

MARTHA: *(to audience)* Yeah, as you can see our bowls are empty. *(shows empty bowl)* We practically survive off air.

TINY TIM: *(to audience)* But we're happy!

MRS. CRATCHIT: *(to audience; overly sappy)* Because we have each other.

TINY TIM: And love!

SCROOGE: *(to GHOST PRESENT)* Seriously, are they for real?

GHOST PRESENT: Yep! Adorable, isn't it?

BOB: A merry Christmas to us all.

TINY TIM: God bless us every one!

SCROOGE: Spirit, tell me if Tiny Tim will live.

GHOST PRESENT: *(puts hands to head as if looking into the future)* Ooooo, not so good...I see a vacant seat in the poor chimney corner, and a crutch without an owner. If SOMEBODY doesn't change SOMETHING, the child will die.

SCROOGE: No, no! Say he will be spared.

GHOST PRESENT: Nope, can't do that, sorry. Unless SOMEONE decides to change... hint, hint.

BOB: A Christmas toast to my boss, Mr. Scrooge! The founder of the feast!

MRS. CRATCHIT: *(angrily)* Oh sure, Mr. Scrooge! If he were here I'd give him a piece of my mind to feast upon. What an odious, stingy, hard, unfeeling man!

BOB: Dear, it's Christmas day. He's not THAT bad. *(Pause)* He's just... THAT sad. *(BOB holds up his bowl)* Come on, kids, to Scrooge! He probably needs it more than us!

MARTHA & TINY TIM: *(holding up their bowls)* To Scrooge!

MRS. CRATCHIT: *(muttering)* Thanks for nothing.

BOB: That's not nice.

MARTHA: And we Cratchits are ALWAYS nice. Read the book, Mom.

MRS. CRATCHIT: Sorry.

(the CRATCHIT FAMILY exits)

SCROOGE: She called me odious! Do I really smell that bad?

GHOST PRESENT: Odious doesn't mean you stink. Although in this case you do... According to the dictionary, odious means "unequivocally detestable." I mean, you are a toad sometimes Mr. Scrooge.

SCROOGE: Wow... that's kind of... mean.

Sneak peek of
Treasure Island for Kids

(enter JIM, TRELAWNEY, and DOCTOR; enter CAPTAIN SMOLLETT from the other side of the stage)

TRELAWNEY: Hello Captain. Are we all shipshape and seaworthy?

CAPTAIN: Trelawney, I don't know what you're thinking, but I don't like this cruise; and I don't like the men.

TRELAWNEY: *(very angry)* Perhaps you don't like the ship?

CAPTAIN: Nope, I said it short and sweet.

DOCTOR: What? Why?

CAPTAIN: Because I heard we are going on a treasure hunt and the coordinates of the island are: *(whispers to DOCTOR)*

DOCTOR: Wow! That's exactly right!

CAPTAIN: There's been too much blabbing already.

DOCTOR: Right! But, I doubt ANYTHING will go wrong!

CAPTAIN: Fine. Let's sail!

(ALL exit)

Act 2 Scene 3

(enter JIM, SILVER, and various other pirates)

SILVER: Ay, ay, mates. You know the song: Fifteen men on the dead man's chest.

ALL PIRATES: Yo-ho-ho and a bottle of rum!

(PIRATES slowly exit)

JIM: *(to the audience)* So, the Hispaniola had begun her voyage to the Isle of Treasure. As for Long John, well, he still is the nicest cook...

SILVER: Do you want a sandwich?

JIM: That would be great, thanks Long John! *(SILVER exits; JIM addresses audience)* As you can see, Long John is a swell guy! Until...

(JIM hides in the corner)

Act 2 Scene 4

(enter SILVER and OTHER PIRATES)

JIM: *(to audience)* I overheard Long John talking to the rest of the pirates.

SILVER: Listen here you, Scallywags! I was with Captain Flint when he hid this treasure. And those cowards have the map. Follow my directions, and no killing, yet. Clear?

DICK: Clear.

SILVER: But, when we do kill them, I claim Trelawney. And remember, dead men don't bite.

GEORGE: Ay, ay, Long John!

(ALL exit but JIM)

JIM: *(to audience)* Oh no! Long John Silver IS the one-legged man that Billy Bones warned me about! I have to tell the others!

(JIM runs offstage)

Sneak peek of
The Tempest for Kids

PROSPERO: Hast thou, spirit, performed to point the tempest that I bade thee?

ARIEL: What? Was that English?

PROSPERO: *(Frustrated)* Did you make the storm hit the ship?

ARIEL: Why didn't you say that in the first place? Oh yeah! I rocked that ship! They didn't know what hit them.

PROSPERO: Why, that's my spirit! But are they, Ariel, safe?

ARIEL: Not a hair perished.

PROSPERO: Woo-hoo! All right. We've got more work to do.

ARIEL: Wait a minute. You're still going to free me, right, Master?

PROSPERO: Oh, I see. Is it sooooo terrible working for me? Huh? Remember when I saved you from that witch? Do you? Remember when that blue-eyed hag locked you up and left you for dead? Who saved you? Me, that's who!

ARIEL: I thank thee, master.

PROSPERO: I will free you in two days, okay? Sheesh. Patience is a virtue, or haven't you heard. Right. Where was I? Oh yeah... I need you to disguise yourself like a sea nymph and then... *(PROSPERO whispers something in ARIEL'S ear)* Got it?

ARIEL: Got it. *(ARIEL exits)*

PROSPERO: *(to MIRANDA)* Awake, dear heart, awake!

(MIRANDA yawns loudly)

PROSPERO: Shake it off. Come on. We'll visit Caliban, my slave.

MIRANDA: The witch's son? You mean the MONSTER! He's creepy and stinky!!!

PROSPERO: Mysterious and sneaky,

MIRANDA: Altogether freaky,

MIRANDA & PROSPERO: He's Caliban the slave!!! *(snap, snap!)*

PROSPERO: *(Calls offstage)* What, ho! Slave! Caliban!

(enter CALIBAN)

CALIBAN: Oh, look it's the island stealers! This is my home! My mother, the witch, left it to me and now you treat me like dirt.

MIRANDA: Oh boo-hoo! I used to feel sorry for you, I even taught you our language, but you tried to hurt me so now we have to lock you in that cave.

CALIBAN: I wish I had never learned your language!

PROSPERO: Go get us wood! If you don't, I'll rack thee with old cramps, and fill all thy bones with aches!

CALIBAN: *(to AUDIENCE)* He's so mean to me! But I have to do what he says. ANNOYING! *(exit CALIBAN)*

(enter FERDINAND led by "invisible" ARIEL)

ARIEL: *(Singing)* Who let the dogs out?! Woof, woof, woof!! *(Spookily)* The watchdogs bark; bow-wow, bow-wow!

FERDINAND: *(Dancing across stage)* Where should this music be? Where is it taking me! What's going on?

Sneak peek of
King Lear for Kids
ACT 1 SCENE 1
KING LEAR's palace

(enter FOOL entertaining the audience with jokes, dancing, juggling, Hula Hooping... whatever the actor's skill may be; enter KENT)

KENT: Hey, Fool!

FOOL: What did you call me?!

KENT: I called you Fool.

FOOL: That's my name, don't wear it out! *(to audience)* Seriously, that's my name in the play!

(enter LEAR, CORNWALL, ALBANY, GONERIL, REGAN, and CORDELIA)

LEAR: The lords of France and Burgundy are outside. They both want to marry you, Cordelia.

ALL: Oooooooo!

LEAR: *(to audience)* Between you and me she IS my favorite child! *(to the girls)* Daughters, I need to talk to you about something. It's a really big deal.

GONERIL & REGAN: Did you buy us presents?

LEAR: This is even better than presents!

GONERIL & REGAN: Goody, goody!!!

CORDELIA: Father, your love is enough for me.

LEAR: Give me the map there, Kent. Girls, I'm tired. I've made a decision: Know that we - and by 'we' I mean 'me' - have divided in three our kingdom...

KENT: Whoa! Sir, dividing the kingdom may cause

chaos! People could die!

FOOL: Well, this IS a tragedy…

LEAR: You worry too much, Kent. I'm giving it to my daughters so their husbands can be rich and powerful… like me!

CORNWALL & ALBANY: Sweet!

GONERIL & REGAN: Wait… what?

CORDELIA: This is olden times. That means that everything we own belongs to our husbands.

GONERIL & REGAN: Olden times stink!

CORDELIA: Truth.

LEAR: So, my daughters, tell your daddy how much you love him. Goneril, our eldest-born, speak first.

GONERIL: Sir, I love you more than words can say! More than outer space, puppies and cotton candy! I love you more than any child has ever loved a father in the history of the entire world, dearest Pops!

CORDELIA: *(to audience)* Holy moly! Surely, he won't be fooled by that. *(to self)* Love, and be silent.

LEAR: Thanks, sweetie! I'm giving you this big chunk of the kingdom here. What says our second daughter, Our dearest Regan, wife to Cornwall? Speak.

REGAN: What she said, Daddy… times a thousand!

CORDELIA: *(to audience)* What?! I love my father more than either of them. But I can't express it in words. My love's more richer than my tongue.

LEAR: Wow, Regan! You get this big hunk of the kingdom. Cordelia, what can you tell me to get this giant piece of kingdom as your own? Speak.

CORDELIA: Nothing, my lord.

LEAR: Nothing?!?

CORDELIA: Nothing.

LEAR: Come on, now. Nothing will come of nothing.

CORDELIA: I love you as a daughter loves her father.

LEAR: Try a little, harder, sweetie!

CORDELIA: Why are my sisters married if they give you all their love?

LEAR: How did you get so mean?

CORDELIA: Father, I will not insult you by telling you my love is like... as big as a whale.

LEAR: *(getting mad)* Fine. I'll split your share between your sisters.

REGAN, GONERIL, & CORNWALL: Yessss!

KENT: Whoa! Let's all just calm down a minute!

LEAR: Peace, Kent! You don't want to mess with me right now. I told you she was my favorite...

GONERIL & REGAN: What!?

LEAR: ...and she can't even tell me she loves me more than a whale? Nope. Now I'm mad.

KENT: Royal Lear, really...

LEAR: Kent, I'm pretty emotional right now! You better not try to talk me out of this...

KENT: Sir, you're acting ... insane.

Sneak peek of
Macbeth for Kids
ACT 2 SCENE 1

(DUNCAN runs on stage and dies with a dagger stuck in him. MACBETH drags his body off and then returns with the bloody dagger. LADY MACBETH enters)

LADY MACBETH: Did you do it?

MACBETH: *(clueless)* Do what?

LADY MACBETH: KILL HIM!

MACBETH: Oh yeah, all done. I have done the deed.

LADY MACBETH: *(pointing at the dagger)* What is that?

MACBETH: What?

LADY MACBETH: Why do you still have the bloody dagger with you?

MACBETH: Ummmmm, I don't know.

LADY MACBETH: Well go put it back!

MACBETH: NO! I'll go no more! I'm scared of the dark, and there is a dead body in there. I am afraid to think what I have done.

LADY MACBETH: Man you are a wimp, give me the dagger. *(LADY MACBETH takes the dagger, exits, and returns)*

LADY MACBETH: All done.

(there is a loud knock at the door)

LADY MACBETH: It's 2am! This really is not a good time for more visitors. *(goes to the door)* Who is it? *(opens door)*

MACDUFF: It is Macduff. I am here to see the king.

MACBETH: He is sleeping in there.

(MACDUFF exits while MACBETH and LADY MACBETH look at each other)

MACDUFF: *(offstage scream)* AGHHHHHHHHHHH – He's dead, he's dead!!! *(MACDUFF enters)*

MACBETH: Who?

MACDUFF: Who do you think? *(they both scream)*

BANQUO: *(BANQUO, MALCOLM, and DONALBAIN enter)* What happened, can't someone get a good night sleep around here?

MACDUFF: The king has been murdered.

MALCOLM & DONALBAIN: Aghhhhhhhh!!!!!!!!

DONALBAIN: We must be next.

MALCOLM: Let's get out of here.

DONALBAIN: I'm heading to Ireland.

MALCOLM: I'm off to England. *(MALCOLM and DONALBAIN exit)*

MACDUFF: Well, since there is no one left to be King, why don't you do it Mac?

LADY MACBETH & MACBETH: Okay. *(LADY MACBETH, MACBETH and MACDUFF exit)*

BANQUO: *(to audience)* I fear, thou play'dst most foully for't. *(MACBETH returns)*

MACBETH: Bank, what are you thinking over there?

BANQUO: Oh, nothing. *(said with a big fake smile)* Gotta go! See ya! *(BANQUO exits)*

Sneak peek of
Taming of the Shrew for Kids

ACT 1 SCENE 1

(Enter LUCENTIO and TRANIO)

LUCENTIO: Well, Tranio, my trusty servant, here we are in Padua, Italy! I can't wait to start studying and learn all about philosophy and virtue!

TRANIO: There is such a thing as too much studying, master Lucentio. We need to remember to have fun too! PARTY!

LUCENTIO: Hey look! Here come some of the locals!

(LUCENTIO and TRANIO move to side of stage; Enter BAPTISTA, KATHERINA, BIANCA, HORTENSIO and GREMIO)

BAPTISTA: Look guys, you know the rules: Bianca can't marry anybody until her older sister, Katherina, is married. That's the plan and I'm sticking to it! If either of you both love Katherina, then please, take her.

KATHERINA: *(Sarcastically)* Wow, thanks Dad.

HORTENSIO: I wouldn't marry her if she were the last woman on earth.

KATHERINA: And I'd rather scratch your face off than marry you!

TRANIO: *(Aside to LUCENTIO)* That wench is stark mad!

BAPTISTA: Enough of this! Bianca, go inside.

BIANCA: Yes, dearest father. My books and

instruments shall be my company. *(She exits)*

KATHERINA: *(At BIANCA)* Goody two-shoes.

BAPTISTA: Bianca is so talented in music, instruments, and poetry! I really need to hire some tutors for her. *(KATHERINA rolls her eyes and sighs)* Good-day everyone! *(BAPTISTA exits)*

KATHERINA: *(Very angry)* AGHHHH!!!! I'm outta here

(Exits opposite direction from her father)

GREMIO: *(Shudders)* Ugh! How could anyone ever want to marry Katherina?!

HORTENSIO: I don't know, but let's find a husband for her.

GREMIO: A husband? A devil!

HORTENSIO: I say a husband.

GREMIO: I say a devil.

HORTENSIO: Alright, alright! There's got to be a guy out there crazy enough to marry her.

GREMIO: Let's get to it!

(Exit GREMIO and HORTENSIO)

LUCENTIO: Oh, Tranio! Sweet Bianca, has stolen my heart! I burn, I pine, I perish! Oh, how I love her!

TRANIO: Whoa, Master! You're getting a little over dramatic, there, Lucentio.

LUCENTIO: Sorry. But my heart is seriously on fire! How am I going to make her fall in love with me if she's not allowed to date anybody? Hmmm...

TRANIO: What if you pretended to be a tutor and went to teach her?

LUCENTIO: YOU ARE BRILLIANT, TRANIO! And because we're new here and no one knows what we look like yet, YOU will pretend to be ME at all the local parties. Quick, let's change clothes.

TRANIO: Here? Now?

LUCENTIO: Yes, Here and now! You can't stop this lovin' feeling! *(Starts singing a love song)*

TRANIO: Please, no singing. I'll do it. *(they exchange hats, socks or jackets)*

Sneak peek of
Oliver Twist for Kids

(enter FAGIN, SIKES, DODGER and NANCY)

DODGER: So that Oliver kid got caught by the police.

FAGIN: He could tell them all our secrets and get us in trouble; we've got to find him. Like, in the next 30 seconds or so.

SIKES: Send Nancy. She's good at getting information quick.

NANCY: Nope. Don't wanna go, Sikes. I like the kid.

SIKES: She'll go, Fagin.

NANCY: No, she won't, Fagin.

SIKES: Yes, she will, Fagin.

NANCY: Fine! Grrrrr….

(NANCY sticks out her tongue at SIKES and storms offstage, then immediately returns)

NANCY: Okay, I checked with my sources and, some gentleman took him home to take care of him.

(NANCY, DODGER and SIKES stare at FAGIN waiting for direction)

FAGIN: Where?

NANCY: I don't know.

FAGIN: WHAT!?!? *(waiting)* Well don't just stand there, GO FIND HIM! *(to audience)* Can't find any good help these days!

(ALL run offstage, bumping into each other in their haste)

ACT 2 SCENE 2

(enter OLIVER)

OLIVER: *(to audience)* I'm out running an errand for Mr. Brownlow to prove that I'm a trustworthy boy. I can't keep hanging out with thieves, right?

(enter NANCY, who runs over to OLIVER and grabs him; SIKES, FAGIN, and DODGER enter shortly after and follow NANCY)

NANCY: Oh my dear brother! I've found him! Oh! Oliver! Oliver!

OLIVER: What!?!? I don't have a sister!

NANCY: You do now, kid. Let's go. *(she drags OLIVER to FAGIN)*

FAGIN: Dodger, take Oliver and lock him up.

DODGER: *(to OLIVER)* Sorry, dude. *(DODGER and OLIVER start to exit)*

OLIVER: Aw, man! Seriously? I just found a good home...

NANCY: Don't be too mean to him, Fagin.

OLIVER: *(as he's exiting)* Yeah, don't be too mean to me, Fagin!

SIKES: *(mimicking NANCY)* Don't be mean, Fagin. Wah, wah, wah. Look, I need Oliver to help me rob a house, okay? He is just the size I want to fit through the window. All sneaky ninja like.

Sneak peek of
Much Ado About Nothing for Kids

ACT 1 SCENE 1

(Enter LEONATO, HERO, and BEATRICE)

LEONATO: *(to audience)* I am The Governor. Governor of Messina, Italy.

HERO: Whatever, Dad. You are always talking about yourself. We know you're "The Governor". We've got it. *(sarcastically)* Governor Leonato.

LEONATO: Now listen to me, Hero. You need to behave yourself. We have guests coming. *(BEATRICE laughs at Hero)* And you Beatrice, you better watch your tongue, because I don't want you getting into a "war of words" with Benedick, again. Got me? Look, here comes a messenger.

(enter MESSENGER)

MESSENGER: Sir, I come to tell you that Don Pedro, the Prince of Arragon, his brother Don John, and his faithful men, Claudio and Benedick, will all be coming soon.

(exit MESSENGER)

HERO: Oh, goodie! I think Claudio is cute!

BEATRICE: Yeah, well, Benedick is NOT! He's always smelly after a battle! Oh look, here comes the smelly one now.

(enter DON JOHN, DON PEDRO, BENEDICK, and CLAUDIO)

LEONATO: Welcome, Don Pedro and friends! You have fought bravely. Please stay and party with us.

DON PEDRO: We will, thank you!

DON JOHN: *(aside and pouting to the audience)* My brother gets all the attention! I hate him!

DON PEDRO: Don John, what are you saying over there?

DON JOHN: Oh nothing, dear brother. *(starts dancing VERY badly)* Just practicing my dance moves for the party!

BEATRICE: *(mockingly to BENEDICK)* So Benedick, you're back again? *(sniffs him)* And, whew! *(plugging her nose with her fingers)* Smelly as usual.

BENEDICK: *(mockingly in a high girl's voice)* "Smelly as usual" You, my dear Beatrice, are a pain as usual. Are you ready to continue our merry war?

BEATRICE: You mean our war of words? You know it!

BENEDICK: You are such a parrot-teacher.

BEATRICE: What did you call me?

BENEDICK: Someone who talks A LOT! What's the matter? Forget your dictionary? You know, *(said slowly as if she doesn't understand English)* PARROT TEACHER.

BEATRICE: Humph! A bird of my tongue is better than a beast of yours!

BENEDICK: I wish my horse had the speed of your tongue!

BEATRICE: *(to audience)* Oh, he makes me sooooo mad! *(BEATRICE stomps her feet like a 4-year old and storms offstage)*

LEONATO: *(to audience)* There's a skirmish of wit between them. *(to all)* Everyone, let's go to my castle.

You know, the castle that belongs to The Governor? *(with two thumbs pointing at himself)*

(ALL exit except CLAUDIO and BENEDICK)

CLAUDIO: *(to BENEDICK)* Hero is sooooooo cute!

BENEDICK: Whoa, did you just say, "cute"? No, no, no, NO! A kitten is cute, a baby is cute, but her? No. With a name like "Hero", she can NOT be cute!

CLAUDIO: Yeah, what about her name?

BENEDICK: Come on. "Hero?" Does she drive the Batmobile and wear a cape, too?

CLAUDIO: Leave her alone because...because...because I think I want to marry her!

BENEDICK: Marry? Whoa, buddy! Listen, I mean, she's a bit..... plain. Actually, I do not like her. And as for marriage, it's overrated, so last year. You'll never catch me getting married. That's right, the single life for me!

CLAUDIO: *(CLAUDIO is day dreamy and lovesick)* She is the sweetest lady that I ever looked on. Could you buy such a jewel?

BENEDICK: *(to audience)* And a case to put her into.

(enter DON PEDRO)

DON PEDRO: Where have you guys been?

BENEDICK: You won't believe this! Lovesick Claudio here wants to marry Hero. Hah! Isn't that hilarious!?

DON PEDRO: Be careful Benedick, my friend. Remember, this is a comedy, and all of Shakespeare's comedies end in marriage.

CLAUDIO: Yeah!

ABOUT THE AUTHOR

BRENDAN P. KELSO, came to writing modified Shakespeare scripts when he was taking time off from work to be at home with his newly born son. "It just grew from there". Within months, he was being asked to offer classes in various locations and acting organizations along the Central Coast of California. Originally employed as an engineer, Brendan never thought about writing. However, his unique personality, humor, and love for engaging the kids with The Bard has led him to leave the engineering world and pursue writing as a new adventure in life! He has always believed, "the best way to learn is to have fun!" Brendan makes his home on the Central Coast of California and loves to spend time with his wife and kids.

CAST AUTOGRAPHS

www.ingramcontent.com/pod-product-compliance
Lightning Source LLC
Chambersburg PA
CBHW070544300426
44113CB00011B/1784